But the angel
said to them, "Do not be afraid.
I bring you good news. It will bring great joy
for all the people. Today in the town of David
a Savior has been born to you.
He is the Messiah, the Lord."

—Luke 2:10–11

ZONDERKIDZ

'Twas the Evening of Christmas
Copyright © 2017 by Glenys Nellist
Illustrations © 2017 by Elena Selivanova

This title is also available as a Zondervan ebook.

Requests for information should be addressed to:

Zonderkidz, 3900 *Sparks Dr. SE, Grand Rapids, Michigan 49546*

ISBN 978-0-310-74553-2

Art direction and design: Ron Huizinga

Printed in China

17 18 19 20 21 /LPC/ 22 21 20 19 18 17 16 15 14 13 12 11 10 9 8 7 6 5 4 3 2 1

This book is dedicated to my encourager, without whom
I would never have been an author.
David, I wouldn't want to spend the evening of
Christmas with anyone else.
—G.N.

With gratitude to my parents. Thank you for making
Christmas the best holiday on earth.
—E.S.

'Twas the Evening of Christmas

Written by Glenys Nellist

Illustrated by Elena Selivanova

ZONDERVAN

'Twas the evening of Christmas, when all through the town,
Every inn was so crowded, no room could be found.
Tired Mary and Joseph, who went door to door,
At last found a place on a small stable floor.

"Thank goodness," said Mary, who tiptoed inside.
The mice saw the donkey and scurried to hide!
The rest of the creatures all cuddled up tight
In hopes that they might have a calm, peaceful night.

The pigeons were nestled all snug in their beds,

While visions of breadcrumbs danced 'round in their heads.

The cows closed their eyes, and the oxen laid down;

The doves cooed so gently; the lambs made no sound.

The moon, through the trees, was just starting to glow
With a glimmer of light on the stable below.
When quite by surprise came a newborn babe's cry
That woke all the animals sleeping nearby.

Up jumped the cows, and the oxen and sheep.

Up popped the pigeons, aroused from their sleep.

They all came to gaze at the small baby boy,

As his mama and papa hugged him with joy.

Now donkeys, now cows, now pigeons, and sheep,
Now oxen and mice in the manger did peep.
His eyes, how they twinkled, his dimples so sweet,
As they nuzzled his fingers and cute little feet.

And out in the fields, taking care of their sheep,

Some shepherds were just getting ready to sleep.

When all of a sudden, they had such a fright,

As a whole choir of angels lit up the night.

But the song of the angels; the words that they said,
Soon let the men know they had nothing to dread.
"Dear shepherds! It's wonderful news that we bring.
A Savior is born—he is Jesus, the King!"

Then back to their slumbers the animals curled,
Amazed at this babe who had entered their world.
As Mary and Joseph got ready for bed,
They snuggled their baby and kissed his sweet head.

They ran to the stable and peeked through the door,
And saw something never imagined before!
There, in a manger, a baby boy lay—
No blankets, no pillow, his bed made of hay.

The stable was filled with a wonderful light
As stars above Bethlehem twinkled so bright.
And high in the heavens, God whispered, "My Son,
You'll bring hope to the world and love everyone."

And to that small stable came three splendid kings
With gifts for the baby—all beautiful things.
They jumped from their camels and knelt at his feet
With their frankincense, gold, and myrrh that smelled sweet.

As Mary laid Jesus, asleep, in the hay,
She thought about all that had happened that day.
The mice heard her whisper, as she tucked him in tight,

"Merry Christmas, my son,

and to all ... a good night."